Play Foundations

Where I Live

Beverley Michael

Acknowledgements

© 2008 Folens Limited, on behalf of the author.

United Kingdom: Folens Publishers, Waterslade House, Thame Road, Haddenham, Buckinghamshire HP17 8NT.

Email: folens@folens.com

Ireland: Folens Publishers, Greenhills Road, Tallaght, Dublin 24.

Email: info@folens.ie

Commissioning Editor: Zoë Nichols
Managing editor: Jane Morgan
Design and layout: Infuze Ltd
Cover design: Infuze Ltd
Illustrations: Theresa Tibbetts
Cover illustration: Cathy Hughes

All Early learning goals and Aspects of learning quoted in this book are taken from *Practice Guidance for the Early Years Foundation Stage* (Department for Education and Skills) and are reproduced under the terms of the Click-Use Licence.

First published 2008 by Folens Limited.

British Library Cataloguing in Publication Data. A catalogue record for this publication is available from the British Library.

ISBN 978-1-85008-335-1

Contents

Introduction

Who the book is for

This book forms part of the *Play Foundations* series which provides guidance for practitioners to set up quality play scenarios or activities with young children. It is written for all those working with three-, four- and five-year-old children in a variety of settings. Although many of the activities are written with nursery or school settings in mind, they can easily be adapted for childminders working with children in their homes. The book will be of particular interest to all those working within the Early Years Foundation Stage framework (EYFS). It will also be useful for parents*.

Learning through play

The activities in this book are based on the EYFS principles:

- Each child is unique and is a competent learner from birth.
- Positive relationships ensure that children learn to be strong and independent.
- Enabling environments play a key role in extending learning and development.
- Learning and development takes many different forms and all areas are connected.

The focus of the activities is on child-initiated learning and the emphasis is on process rather than product. There are suggestions for using your guidance, your language and your support to promote the children's learning as they explore and play. Many of the activities can be enjoyed outside. Being outside has a positive impact on children's sense of well-being and can help all aspects of development.

How to use this book

The book is divided into five chapters, each focusing on a different aspect of the home and local environment, with each chapter demonstrating how linked activities can support all areas of children's learning and development.

The chapters are:

- My home
- Who lives in my home?
- Things I do in my home
- My neighbourhood
- Where do I live?

The activities

Each chapter has six activities, each focusing on either one or two Areas of learning and development. The activities give a specific Early learning goal for each learning focus. Most of the activities are designed for small groups of around four children, but in cases where individuals require more support, it may be relevant to work with just one or two children.

Each activity is divided into sections to make it easy to follow:

- To help to plan *Enabling environments*, there is a section on *Setting up*, outlining the resources needed and how to set up.
- *Getting started* describes how to organise the actual activity.
- *Let's talk!* provides ideas for talking with the children about their experiences including questions that could be asked and how to differentiate language to suit the children's varying abilities. There are also suggestions for making the most of assessment opportunities.

- Recognising *A unique child*, and *Positive relationships*, means making sure that self-esteem, confidence and relationships remain positive and there are *Top tips* for doing so.
- The *Differentiation* section includes ideas for personalising the learning by adjusting each activity to make it easier for those children needing support or more challenging for others. This section will also be useful for planning inclusive activities for those children who have special or additional needs.
- *Further ideas* for each activity suggest ways of extending and enhancing learning and development opportunities.
- Photocopiable activity sheets are provided in the book and they can also be printed from the CD-ROM. They are intended to enhance children's play or to create game scenarios.
- Every activity page lists relevant resources on the CD-ROM.

The importance of ICT

Nowadays, young children are becoming increasingly familiar with using ICT as part of their everyday experiences. Stories, rhymes and songs can be enjoyed through television and computer programs, and many early years settings have interactive whiteboard facilities. Children are surrounded by texts that combine images, sounds and words both on screen and paper and they need to learn to read images as well as print. The CD-ROM that accompanies this book provides opportunities for children to explore and become familiar with visual text, photographic and drawn still images, moving images, sound and colour.

Using the CD-ROM

The CD-ROM has been designed for children to use with adult support.

Claude Cat

Claude Cat gives instructions or asks questions which are designed to encourage children to verbalise their observations, ideas and understanding. This will help you to assess whether they need further support or challenge.

The main menu

This screen has the option to select a theme.

The theme menu

When the theme screen is displayed, you have the option of selecting different resources, for example, an interactive picture, story, rhyme or song, by clicking on the appropriate icon:

| Songs | Rhymes | Stories | Activity sheets | Interactive pictures | Photos (some have sound) | Film clips |

* Whenever the term 'parent' is used this is taken to include parents and/or the children's primary carers.

Planning chart

Use this chart to help with your planning. Each activity focuses on either one or two Area(s) of learning and development. These are highlighted by the stars shown on the chart. The Areas of learning and development are divided into 'aspects' and the aspect(s) for each activity are also provided on the chart. On the activity pages you will also find an 'Early learning goal' objective for each activity.

The following key is used on the activity pages:

 PSED: Personal, social and emotional development

 CLL: Communication, language and literacy

 PSRN: Problem solving, reasoning and numeracy

 KUW: Knowledge and understanding of the world

 PD: Physical development

 CD: Creative development

Activities		Areas of learning and development						
My home	Page	PSED	CLL	PSRN	KUW	PD	CD	Aspect of learning
Architects	10						★	Exploring media and materials
				★				Shape, space and measures
The house that Jack built	11				★			Designing and making
Knock on my door	12			★				Numbers as labels and for counting
Be careful!	14	★						Self-confidence and self-esteem
Moving home	16					★		Using equipment and materials
Home furnishings	17				★			Exploration and investigation
			★					Language for communication
Who lives in my home?	Page	PSED	CLL	PSRN	KUW	PD	CD	Aspect of learning
Spoon families	18		★					Language for thinking
Family portrait	19						★	Exploring media and materials
Whose hat is that?	20	★						Sense of community
Family days	22				★			Time
Happy families	23			★				Calculating
Pets at home	24					★		Using equipment and materials

Things I do in my home	Page	PSED	CLL	PSRN	KUW	PD	CD	Aspect of learning
I get dressed	26	★						Self-care
							★	Developing imagination and imaginative play
Tidy time	28			★				Shape, space and measures
I play with my toys	30						★	Creating music and dance
I help to clean	31		★					Language for communication
						★		Movement and space
I eat my meals	32					★		Health and bodily awareness
I play in my garden	33				★			Exploration and investigation

My neighbourhood	Page	PSED	CLL	PSRN	KUW	PD	CD	Aspect of learning
Our street	34				★			Place
Tidy neighbourhood	35	★						Behaviour and self-control
					★			Place
My friends	36					★		Movement and space
		★						Making relationships
Going to school	38			★				Shape, space and measures
People around us	40		★					Language for communication
							★	Develop imagination and imaginative play
Traffic on our street	41						★	Being creative – responding to experiences, expressing and communicating ideas

Where do I live?	Page	PSED	CLL	PSRN	KUW	PD	CD	Aspect of learning
Castles in the air	42						★	Developing imagination and imaginative play
				★				Shape, space and measures
I live in the sea	44				★			Exploration and investigation
				★				Numbers as labels and for counting
Cave homes	45					★		Movement and space
			★					Language for communication
Homes in cold places	46		★					Language for communication
I live in a shoe	47			★				Numbers as labels and for counting
Gingerbread house	48	★						Making relationships
				★				Shape, space and measures

Assessment ideas

Young children are individuals first, each with a unique profile of abilities. All the planning that we do should flow from the observations that we make on an on-going basis and these will help us to understand and consider their current interests, development and learning.

How to assess children

Observing children during their daily routines allows us to note their responses in different situations and to different people. In some settings, a specific Area of learning and development is targeted and the key person is asked to observe what stage the children in their care have reached over the next day or week, revisiting that Area from time to time. Others use sticky notes in order to capture relevant observations. These can be collated later by a key person and entered into the ongoing records for the child. Others make use of photos, daily diaries, activity feedback sheets or tracking records to capture the children's progress at different times. There is no prescribed method and you will find methods that suit your practice and the children and families concerned.

Planning for assessment

Through assessment you can see what stages the children have reached in their learning and development and therefore work out the best resources, opportunities and activities to plan next. Sometimes this might involve planning a specific activity to enable the child to take their learning that little bit further, or it may be necessary to plan a similar activity in order to reinforce learning further before moving on. Sometimes it will simply mean providing the right opportunities and observing the children as they play and learn independently. You will find a mixture of adult-led and child-led activities in the activity chapters with suggestions for you to observe and assess the children within the *Let's talk!* sections of each page.

Using your assessments

Once you have observed the children at play, analyse your observations and highlight the children's achievements or their need for further support. Assessments are the decisions you make using what you have observed about each child's development and learning. You are asked to involve parents and carers as part of the ongoing observation and assessment process and it is also helpful to share your plans for the short-term (a week) and long-term (a term) planning. Your planning should always follow the same pattern – observe, analyse and reflect, then use what you have found out to plan next steps in the child's learning. In this way you can personalise the children's learning and make the most of their strengths, interests and needs.

The 'Look, listen and note' approach of the EYFS is a helpful tool when deciding what to observe and how. On the next page, this format has been applied to children learning about *Where I Live* so that you can begin to think about how your assessment and observations of children within this theme can feed back into your planning. For each of the five chapter headings, there are ideas for what you should look out for especially.

Observation hints

Here are some suggestions to help focus your observation and assessments when children are learning about *Where I Live*.

Chapter heading	Look, listen and note
My home	Observe children's physical and design skills as they build and construct houses. Can they select and improvise using a variety of materials?
	Listen to the mathematical language children use as they build and draw various homes, for example, door numbers and shapes of roofs and windows.
	Make a note of children's understanding of home situations which may prove a danger to their safety.
Who lives in my home?	Observe children painting and drawing family members. Are they representational figures?
	Listen to the children's responses as they talk about who lives with them in their home.
	Make a note of those children who re-enact family situations, for example, during role-play or when using puppets.
Things I do in my home	Observe those children who can dress and undress independently during role-play activities.
	Listen to children's language skills as they talk about their favourite foods and toys. Are they developmentally appropriate?
	Note those children who join in with group activities, for example, when playing with noisy toys and singing songs and rhymes about cleaning and tidying up.
My neighbourhood	Observe those children who make friends with others in the group. Can they take turns and share?
	Listen to whether children ask suitable questions of adult visitors from the local neighbourhood. Are they attentive?
	Note children who can identify the importance of keeping their neighbourhood tidy and understand the consequences of dropping litter.
Where do I live?	Observe children's reactions as they make mini igloos. Are they able to talk about 'melting' and 'freezing'?
	Listen to the language used by the children as they re-enact stories and rhymes about homes, for example, during Jack and the Giant role-play, making caves in the sand and houses from food.
	Note and write down counting skills used by children, such as when counting objects.

CD-ROM resources

A home

Early learning goals

Explore colour, texture, shape, form and space in two or three dimensions.

Use language such as 'circle' or 'bigger' to describe the shape and size of solids and flat shapes.

ENABLING ENVIRONMENTS

Setting up

Look at pictures and photos of the different types of homes that children might live in. Include as many different homes as possible, for example, flats, semi-detached, travellers' caravans, bungalows, cottages, terraces, bed-sits, farmhouses and houseboats.

Getting started

- The children will have many different experiences of housing. Gather the children together and talk about the various types, especially those that children may not be familiar with. Discuss the photo of the house on the CD-ROM and talk about its appearance and who might live there. Any home needs to provide shelter and warmth and most usually have doors and windows. Show the children a cardboard box painted to represent a house but minus a door. Choose a small soft toy and pretend it wants to get into the house. What is missing? Cut a door in the house for the toy to enter.
- Explain that an architect is a person who designs homes (look at some blueprints if you can find some). Encourage the children to become 'architects' and draw their own home, using pencils and markers of various thicknesses. See if they can think carefully of their own home as they draw. When they have finished, invite them to use their imagination to design a home for a nursery rhyme or story character such as Humpty Dumpty.

Let's talk!

Ask, *What colour is the door on your house? How many windows does your home have? What shape is your roof?* For children needing support, ask *Can you draw a picture of your home?* For children requiring challenge, ask *How will Humpty Dumpty get into his house?* Notice if the children are able to hold pencils and markers correctly and use rulers to make straight lines.

A UNIQUE CHILD

POSITIVE RELATIONSHIPS

Top tip

Be sensitive to the housing arrangements of the children in your particular setting and include reference to the types of homes the children may be familiar with.

Differentiation

Provide an assortment of coloured paper shapes such as squares, triangles and rectangles for less confident children to use to make their home. Challenge children to use rulers, set squares and shape templates to obtain straight edges.

Further ideas

- Draw houses using a simple drawing package on the computer.
- Place all the drawings on a large piece of paper, mural fashion, to create a town.

The house that Jack built

CD-ROM resources

 The house that Jack built

 Building site

Early learning goal

Build and construct with a wide range of objects, selecting appropriate resources, and adapting their work where necessary.

LEARNING AND DEVELOPMENT

ENABLING ENVIRONMENTS

Setting up

Set up the sand tray outdoors. Place small PE cones, if available, around the sand tray to warn that 'builders' are at work. Provide hard hats for the children to wear.

Getting started

- Invite a local builder into your setting to show the children some of the tools he uses in his work. He may bring a bag of sand, a drill and a trowel, for example. Try to borrow different types of bricks, roofing tiles, floor tiles and plastic guttering to show the children. Discuss what each is used for and let the children examine them closely. Look at the video of the building site on the CD-ROM and watch a builder at work.
- Invite the children to play in the sand using toy builders' tools (saws, trowels, hammers, plastic brick moulds, spades and so on). Encourage them to build walls of sand using plastic brick moulds. Introduce some construction toys to the sand play. Challenge the children to build different types of houses in the sand using the various materials.
- Give the children the opportunity to show their houses to the rest of the group and photograph them as a permanent record of their construction. Say the rhyme 'The house that Jack built' (on the CD-ROM) with the children as they look at the houses. Display the photos with the builders' names: 'This is the house that (Amanda) built', for example.

Let's talk!

Ask, *Can you build a house in the sand? What are the best type of bricks to use? What would you use to make the strongest house?* For children needing challenge, ask *Is it easier to build on a soft or hard base? Can you make a hard base in the sand?* Note whether the children can build carefully and methodically – do they realise that a flat base is needed for building houses with bricks?

UNIQUE CHILD

Top tip

Encourage the children to collaborate with one another, respecting all the constructions.

POSITIVE RELATIONSHIPS

Differentiation

Let children who need more support use small building bricks and sing 'This is the way I build my house' to the tune of 'Here we go round the mulberry bush' as they build. Challenge children to build a high wall for a soft toy to sit on and fall off like Humpty Dumpty.

Further ideas

- Create brick and stone wall or roof tile patterns using potato-printing technique.

Knock on my door

Setting up

Discuss with the children the importance of knowing their address (number and street name) in case they get lost. Encourage all the children to be able to repeat their address.

Getting started

- Ask the children to tell you the colour of their front door and whether it has a letter-box, bell, number or handle on it. Can they describe their door? Is it made of wood? Does it have any glass in it? Look at the photo of the door on the CD-ROM and talk about any of the features they can see.
- Give each child a small, rectangular cardboard box (an empty tissue box works well) and stand it on end. Ask them to paint it the same colour as their own front door, and when it is dry, paint the number of their house on the door. Cut out a letter-box shape in the door for the children, large enough for a small envelope.
- Place all the boxes in a row, on the floor, a table, or outdoors on a fine day. Invite the children to write a short note (scribe for them where necessary) and place the letters in small envelopes. Ask them to write their name and the number of their house on their envelope. Let the children take turns to play postman and deliver their letter through the doors. Encourage them to say the number names on their doors as they do so.

Let's talk!

Ask, *Can you tell me your address? Whose door is next to yours? How many doors are there altogether?* For children needing more support, ask *Where do you live?* For children needing challenge, ask *What number is (Kim's) door?* Notice if the children can say their house number and street name. Do they say and recognise that number while posting letters?

Top tip

Respect the different types of homes the children may live in. Children who have no house number in their address can use a fictional number for this activity.

Differentiation

Reduce the number of doors to five for children needing more support, perhaps with a small photo of the child on their door. Children who require challenge can take turns to be the postman and deliver all the children's letters through the doors.

Further ideas

- Give each child a copy of the activity sheet 'Knock, knock!' (photocopy page 13 or print from the CD-ROM) to complete. Talk about what colour front door each child has at home.

Knock, knock!

Can you colour three doors red? Colour two doors blue and one door yellow.

Be careful!

CD-ROM resources

Safety in the kitchen

Early learning goal

Have a developing awareness of their own needs, views and feelings, and be sensitive to the needs, views and feelings of others.

Setting up

Set up the role-play area as a kitchen with areas of possible danger in mind – cooking utensils, cupboards containing clean, empty cleaning-product bottles, a toy kettle and so on. Include some containers of things that are safe to drink. Create some 'hazard triangles' (either cards featuring a red triangle or triangles cut from red card) which can be stuck in place with an easily removable fixing, such as masking tape, and place them in a wallet on the wall.

Getting started

- Talk about safety in the home with the group. Have any of the children hurt themselves in their home? Can they talk about their experiences? Encourage them to think about things which might be dangerous, such as leaving their toys at the top of the stairs, boiling saucepans, kettles or hot ovens, and how to avoid danger from plugs in sockets, fires, matches or knives. Discuss the way we are told that something is dangerous. The children may be told *no!*, *stop!* or *don't touch that!* and these words may be said loudly. Explain that this is because they need to stop doing something quickly otherwise they may get hurt.
- A red triangle is sometimes used as a warning signal. Talk about some of the dangers which might be found in a kitchen. Can they identify any hazards in the role-play kitchen area? Encourage children to use the hazard triangles to mark them out during their play. Make it clear that children should never drink anything that they do not know to be safe.
- Give each child a copy of the activity sheet 'Safety in the kitchen' (photocopy page 15 or print from the CD-ROM) and ask them to stick red warning triangles on any potentially dangerous areas they can see in the picture. Provide some triangles cut from red paper.

Let's talk!

For children needing support, ask *When do we know something is safe to drink?* For children requiring challenge, ask *Can you think of a safe place to store dangerous containers and medicines?* Note the children who can explain why certain situations in the home can be dangerous and use the knowledge in their role-play.

Top tip

Show sensitivity when discussing accidents or occasions when children have been hurt in the home. Talk on a one-to-one basis if the child prefers.

Differentiation

Children who need more support can sort the empty containers into 'you can drink this' and 'you can't drink this' categories. Challenge children by asking them to help you make a poster showing safety rules for the setting (tidying toys, don't run, mopping spillages).

Further ideas

- Place posters in the washroom explaining the importance of washing hands after visiting the toilet and before eating.

Safety in the kitchen

What can you see that could be dangerous in this kitchen?

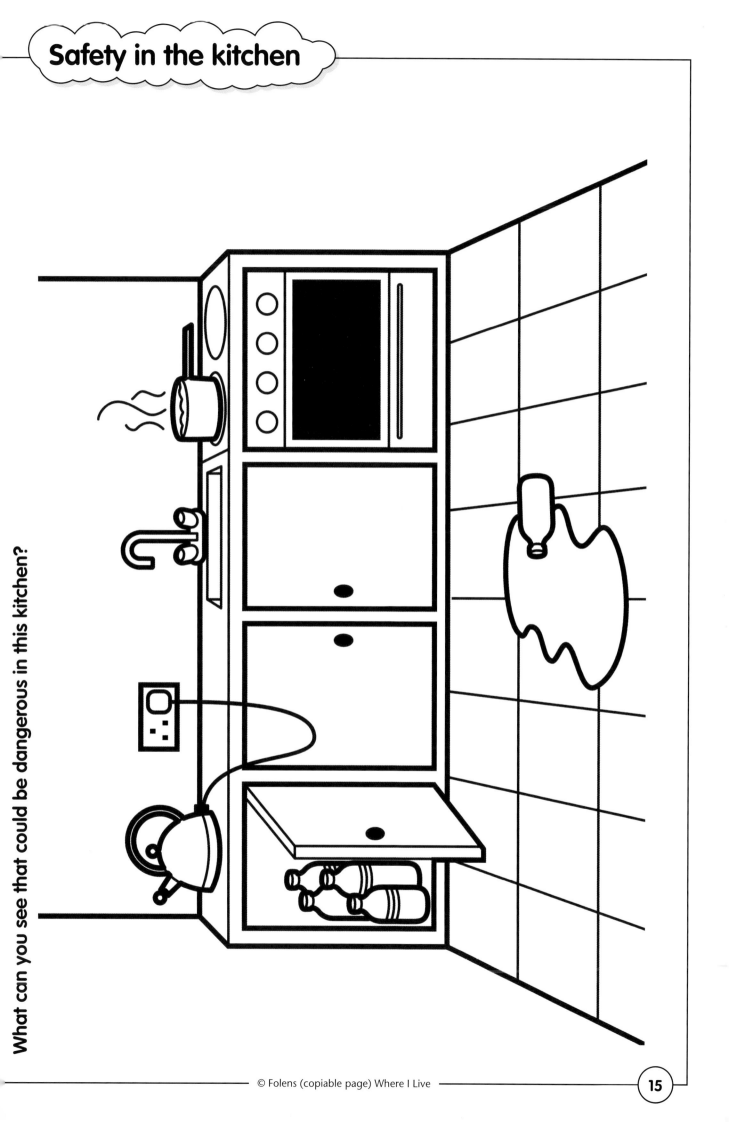

Moving home

Setting up

Begin by asking the children if any of them have ever moved from one home to another. Read a book about moving house such as *Moving Molly* by Shirley Hughes (Red Fox Picture Books) as a useful start for children who have not been through the process.

Getting started

- Explain to the children that you are going to move house by packing up everything in the role-play area and creating a new house outside. Can they choose a place outdoors that they think would be suitable? Ask them to build the walls of the house using large building blocks, cardboard boxes, plastic crates or by draping blankets over a climbing frame or clothes-horse. Adults should move any large furniture items.
- Ask for suggestions about the best way of packing up and carrying the small items outdoors. Provide a variety of shopping bags, boxes and small suitcases and show children how to wrap items in newspaper to protect them. They will find that if they pack the bags neatly and carefully they can fit in more items.
- Can the children plan how to move any heavy boxes or bags to the new house? They may decide to push or pull the boxes but placing them on wheeled toys, such as trolleys, push and pull trucks, cars, tractors and trailers, scooters, prams and pushchairs makes it much easier, especially if they work co-operatively. Let the children unpack and arrange the role-play items in the new house, and enjoy playing with familiar objects in new surroundings for a few days.

Let's talk!

Ask, *How many things can you move in your suitcase? What did you use to get that suitcase to the new house?* For children needing support, ask *Did you pull your truck or push your truck to the new house?* For children requiring challenge, ask *How can you stop items from getting broken?* Notice if the children used the wheeled toys to successfully move items outdoors.

Top tip

For some children, constant moving may be a common occurrence. It may be a situation which they are reluctant to discuss. Encourage them to share their experiences. Do not let children attempt to move heavy items.

Differentiation

Let children who need support move towels, clothes and other fabric items in prams and pushchairs. Challenge children to find other ways to move large cardboard boxes, such as pulling them with ropes or rolling them along large cardboard tubes.

Further ideas

- Ask the children to think where they would live if they had to move home. Listen to the rhyme 'Where should I live?' on the CD-ROM, joining in and making appropriate animal actions.

Home furnishings

Colourful cushions

Early learning goals

Interact with others, negotiating plans and activities and taking turns in conversation.

Investigate objects and materials by using all of their senses as appropriate.

Setting up

Make a collection of wallpaper, carpet and home furnishing fabric samples (ask shops if they have any out-of-date sample books they could donate). Cut 24 rectangular shapes (approximately 10cm x 20cm) from thick card.

Getting started

- Start by showing the children the collection of home furnishing samples. Try to find interesting repeat patterns which will appeal to children, particularly those wallpapers and fabrics aimed for a child's bedroom. Talk about the different colours, patterns and textures. Can they see any patterns which are the same? Are there any shapes they can identify? Look at the photo of cushions on the CD-ROM and talk about the colours and patterns. Encourage the children to talk about any wallpaper, curtains and carpets in their home. What colour and design is it?

- Cut the wallpaper, carpet and fabric samples into twenty-four 10cm x 20cm rectangles (two of each design). Ask the children to paste them on to the cards and leave them to dry. Place all the cards on a table face down and invite four children to take turns at turning over two at a time. If a child turns over two cards which are exactly the same they keep the matching pair, otherwise replace them face down again in the same position and let the next child have a turn. Encourage them to discuss the whereabouts of the cards with each other, awaiting their turn. When all the cards have been paired, ask the group to count which child has found the most pairs.

Let's talk!

Ask, *Where do you think there might be another card that matches? Can you say if the card is made of carpet, wallpaper, or fabric material?* For children needing support, ask *What colour is the wallpaper card you have just turned over?* For children requiring challenge, ask *Can you shuffle the cards and place them face down ready for another game?* Notice if the children can take turns fairly while playing the game.

Top tip

Try to include all the children by asking if they could bring scraps or offcuts of fabric, wallpaper or carpet from their own home to include on the cards which they can enjoy recognising.

Differentiation

Play with just six matching pairs of cards to support children, using patterns which are easily distinguishable. Challenge other children to play with a larger number of cards.

Further ideas

- Let children use sponge shapes to make repeat designs on the reverse of a length of wallpaper.

Who lives in my home? Spoon families

CD-ROM resources

Sock puppets

Early learning goal

Use language to imagine and recreate roles and experiences.

Setting up

Create a puppet theatre outdoors by hanging two blankets over a length of rope tied between two chairs, like a pair of curtains. Make a collection of plastic and wooden spoons of all shapes and sizes. Collect some photos of family groups – children could bring in their own family picture.

Getting started

- Look at a photo of a family group and discuss the different members. Introduce the collection of spoons to the children. Ask them if they can identify which are made of plastic and which are made of wood. Can they say what the spoons might be used for – for example, taking medicine, eating a yogurt or stirring a cake mix? Ask the children to choose a spoon which could make a good 'daddy' puppet (such as a large wooden spoon) or a 'baby puppet' (a teaspoon). Let them choose enough spoons to represent each member of their own family. Provide a range of flesh-tone colours (acrylic paint) so children can paint the faces but leave the tip of the handle unpainted for handling. Wooden spoons may require two coats of paint.
- When the spoons are dry, ask the children to draw their family member's face on the back of the spoon with felt pens. They might want to add hair using wool or straw. Let them choose scraps of material for clothing and fasten them around the spoons with tape or elastic bands. Encourage the children to play with their spoon puppets using the puppet theatre outdoors, recreating family situations and acting out family-based stories.

Let's talk!

Ask, *What do you think this puppet might say? What might happen next in your story?* For children needing support, ask *Which member of your family is this puppet meant to be?* For children requiring challenge, ask *Why do you think your new 'baby brother' puppet might cry?* Observe whether children can tell of an event which may have happened using the puppets to speak for them.

Top tip

Be sensitive to family circumstances. Encourage children to make imaginary characters if they are unwilling to create family-based ones. Help individuals by playing alongside them, adding suggestions to enhance play.

Differentiation

Help children requiring support when fastening the fabric clothing. Children needing challenge can make a spoon that is sad on one side and happy on the other, or asleep on one side and awake on the other.

Further ideas

- Look at the photo 'Sock puppets' on the CD-ROM and talk about how the puppets are made. Parents can use socks as puppets with the children at home.
- Use spoons to create animal puppets – a tiger, lion or elephant.

Family portrait

CD-ROM resources

Family portrait

Early learning goal

Explore colour, texture, shape, form and space in two or three dimensions.

LEARNING AND DEVELOPMENT

ENABLING ENVIRONMENTS

Setting up
Read stories featuring families with the children, such as the *Happy Families* series by Janet and Allan Ahlberg (Puffin). Look at the painting 'Family portrait' on the CD-ROM and talk about the family and their appearance.

Getting started
- Encourage the children to talk about who lives with them in their house. Talk about any family customs or religious traditions which take place in their home, such as mealtimes, Ramadan fasting, the Jewish Sabbath, and so on. Provide the children with large sheets of paper and paint in a variety of flesh tones and ask them to paint a picture showing all the people they live with. Encourage the children to be as accurate as possible in their paintings, giving family members the correct colour hair and skin tone. They may wish to add fabric scraps as clothes or straw, wool or wood shavings to represent hair when their painting is dry.
- When the children have finished frame the pictures and display them, with the child's name clearly shown, in a 'family portrait gallery'. Ask each child to name and talk about each family member in their painting to the rest of the group.

Let's talk!
Ask, *Who is the smallest in your family? What is your sister wearing in the picture?* For children requiring support, ask *What colour is your mum's hair? Can you paint it that colour?* For children needing challenge, ask *Can you make your paint darker or lighter?* Note if the children are able to draw and paint representational figures of family members. Are they willing to explore the paint to create the effects they require?

A UNIQUE CHILD

POSITIVE RELATIONSHIPS

Top tip
Every child has some experience of a family and all families vary, ranging from extended family members to single-parent families. Become familiar with the family circumstances of the children in your group. Deal sensitively with any issues that may arise on a one-to-one basis.

Differentiation
Support children through the painting activity, offering suggestions if necessary and accepting their results. Encourage children requiring challenge to add more details to their pictures, such as things that are important to their family.

Further ideas
- Ask children to paint a picture of their home. Hang it from a coat hanger and suspend pictures of the people who live in the house underneath in a 'who lives in my house' mobile.
- Explain that a self-portrait is a picture of yourself. Let children create a self-portrait by looking at themselves in a safety mirror and painting what they see.

Whose hat is that?

Early learning goal

Understand that people have different needs, views, cultures and beliefs, that need to be treated with respect.

LEARNING AND DEVELOPMENT

ENABLING ENVIRONMENTS

Setting up

Make a collection of hats which may be worn by various members of a family (baby bonnets, hard hats, flat caps, baseball caps, woollen hats, sun hats, wedding hats, rain hats).

Getting started

- Gather the children together in a circle outside and introduce the collection of hats. Have fun trying them on as they guess which member of a family might wear a particular hat. Place the hats in the middle of the circle and choose one to pass around from one child to another. As they do so, encourage them to say the following rhyme altogether to the tune of 'Pop goes the weasel':

    Here's a hat and there's a hat
    Pass it round the circle
    Take a hat and put it on
    Now I'm a (… baby sister)

    After the line 'Take a hat and put it on' stop and ask the child left holding the hat to put it on their head and finish the rhyme by saying which particular member of a family might wear a hat like that.
- Keep all the hats in a hat box and place it in the role-play area. Encourage the children to use the hats to role-play the different people in their family. Take the hat box outside and let the children wear the hats during their outdoor play.
- After the activities introduce the idea that some people wear special headwear because of their beliefs.

Let's talk!

Ask, *When would someone wear this hat? Does your mum or dad wear a special hat?* For children requiring more support, ask *Who do you think would wear a hat like this?* For children needing challenge, ask *Can you think of any other types of hats?* Note if the children can distinguish the different types of hats and who might wear them.

A UNIQUE CHILD

Top tip

Include headwear worn by children from varying ethnic or religious backgrounds by asking those children to show hats or headwear they may wear on particular occasions to the rest of the group.

POSITIVE RELATIONSHIPS

Differentiation

Limit the hats to six easily definable ones while playing the game. Add hats to the collection which represent occupations – police officers, firefighters, nurses and so on. Add these occupations to the end of the rhyme: *Now I'm a firefighter*, for example, and distinguish between these and family hats.

Further ideas

- Give each child a copy of the activity sheet 'Family hats' (photocopy from page 21 or print from the CD-ROM). Cut out the hats and match them with the different family members.

Family hats

Cut out the hats and match them to each member of the family. Which is the best hat for each person?

rain hat

bonnet

sun hat

bobble hat

Family days

CD-ROM resources

The best of friends

Early learning goal

Find out about past and present events in their own lives, and in those of their families and other people they know.

Setting up

Set up a special 'story chair' in your story corner for visitors and add cushions and drapes. Send a letter home with the children, asking for volunteers from family members who would be willing to come and enjoy a cup of tea and a biscuit with a small group of children and bring a favourite storybook to share. Prepare an invitation (in a 'teapot' or 'cup and saucer' shape) leaving spaces to fill in names and times.

Getting started

- Invite the children to talk about who, if anyone, reads stories to them at home. Explain that you are going to invite members of their families to tea in your setting at story times. Set aside 15 minutes once a week and select one of the volunteers. Help the children to fill in an invitation and send it to them. On the day, let the child whose family member has been invited welcome the visitor and show them around, then introduce them to the rest of the group. Invite no more than six children to sit quietly and attentively and listen to the story read by the visitor and allow time afterwards for them to ask any questions.
- Invite storytellers to bring any interesting objects they may have to show to the children, an item from the past or favourite old toy, for example, and say why it is special. Some may like to play an instrument, talk about an old family photograph or share a celebration.

Let's talk!

Ask, *What was the book about? What did David's grandmother bring to show you today?* For children requiring support, ask *Do you know who read the story to you today?* For children needing challenge, ask *What did Sofia's sister tell you that she did on her birthday yesterday?* Notice which children sit and listen attentively.

Top tip

Provide a suitable storybook for visitors and discuss any queries that they may have beforehand. Be aware that some children may not have a family member who lives in their house who is able to volunteer – so include aunts, uncles and grandparents.

Differentiation

Limit story group numbers to four with children who need more support and make sure the book is appropriate for their age. Challenge children to 'write' or decorate a short note of thanks to the storyteller.

Further ideas

- Listen to the story 'The best of friends' on the CD-ROM.

Happy families

CD-ROM resources

Puppet families

 Early learning goal

Use language such as 'more' or 'less' to compare two numbers.

Setting up

Create a town by drawing streets, using felt pens or crayons, on a large sheet of card. With larger groups, use the reverse of a length of wallpaper to make a frieze of town streets.

Getting started

- Look at the photo on the CD-ROM showing two puppet families and talk about how many members there are. In groups of four, invite the children to draw small pictures on card of all the people who live in their house, including pets, and cut them out carefully. (So that the children know whose families belong to who they can either write their name on each one or mark a particular colour on all their family members.) Give each child an envelope and ask them to draw windows and a door on the flap side using felt pens. They can now place their family characters in the envelope house. Encourage the children to introduce their family characters to the rest of the group, counting how many members live in their house.

- Open up the envelope flap so that it forms the roof of the house, leaving the pocket at the front. The children can now glue their envelope houses along the streets of the town. They may also enjoy drawing and cutting out cars to park outside their house, trees in a park and so on. Let the children play with the town map, taking their family characters to school, the park or the shops. When they have finished they can count and sort the characters and replace them correctly in their houses.

Let's talk!

Ask, *Look at Leon's family – do 'more' people or 'less' people live in your house?* For support, ask *Who lives in your house?* For children requiring challenge, ask *How many people are left in your house if two go to the park?* Note which children can compare the number of members in each family.

Top tip

Before the activity, find out as much as you can about the size of families within the group. Ask if any parents could send a family photo for their child to share with the rest of the group. Remind all the children that whether there are two or twelve people, they still make a family.

Differentiation

Cut out the small family figures for children requiring support and try to keep family numbers to five or less. Challenge more able children to match numbers on envelope houses with the different families who live inside.

Further ideas

- Let each child plant a small branch or twig in a plastic pot as a 'family tree' and stick their family characters on the branches.

Pets at home

CD-ROM resources

 Puppy and kitten

 This is the way my dog can jump

My pets

Early learning goal

 Handle tools, objects, construction and malleable materials safely and with increasing control.

Setting up
Look at a collection of books and photos showing various types of pets with the children.

Getting started
- Look at the photo of a puppy and kitten on the CD-ROM and talk about who has pets. Not all homes will have a pet so involve those children by asking them to think of a pet they would like to have. Provide the children, in groups of four, with a small ball of play dough, clay or similar and ask them to try to create their pet. Encourage them to roll small lengths of material between their palms to make legs and tails and pinch and squeeze ears using fingers. Clay tools can be used to create eyes in the model and also to make patterns representing fur, scales or feathers.
- Photocopy from page 25 or print out from the CD-ROM the activity sheet 'My pets'. Cut out the pet shapes and enlarge them individually, so that each child has an animal shape that corresponds to their pet. Ask them to write their name on it and use it to display their models on a table for everyone to see. Children with a pet not represented on the activity sheet can draw their own pet shape. Encourage the children to find out information from the display, such as the most popular pet, or how many children own a cat.

Let's talk!
What is the best way to join your cat's legs to the body? For children requiring support, ask *What pet are you going to make? What do you need to do first?* For children needing challenge, ask *Can you make your pet stand up on legs? Are the legs strong enough to hold the weight of the body?*

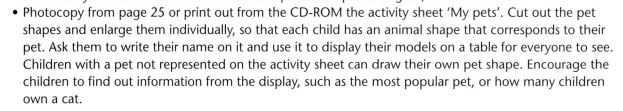

Top tip
Be aware that pets are not suitable for all families, due to allergies, space or lifestyles, but all children should be included by modelling an imaginary pet or one they would like to own.

Differentiation
Provide pet-shaped cutters for children needing support, using rolling pins to flatten the play dough before cutting. Children requiring challenge can leave the clay and play dough models to dry and harden and then paint them.

Further ideas
- Listen to the rhyme 'This is the way my dog can jump' on the CD-ROM and encourage children to join in with actions.

My pets

CD-ROM resources

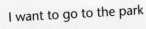 Washing line

 I want to go to the park

Early learning goals

 Dress and undress independently and manage their own personal hygiene.

Use their imagination in art and design, music, dance, imaginative and role-play and stories.

LEARNING AND DEVELOPMENT

ENABLING ENVIRONMENTS

Setting up

Gather together a selection of clothes that could be worn on different occasions or at certain times of the year (in the snow, to the park, on the beach, to a party, going to bed and so on). Listen to the rhyme 'I want to go to the park' on the CD-ROM and decide with the children which clothes to wear.

Getting started

• Gather the group together and invite each child to describe the clothes that they put on when they got dressed at home that morning. Show the children your collection of clothes, discuss how you would put them on and how the clothes fasten. Place the new clothes in the role-play area or set up a clothing rail in the outdoor play area. Provide a large, safe mirror for the children to look at themselves as they try them on. Encourage them to say when they would wear certain types of clothing and use this to lead their role-play. Suggest that the children help each other with fastenings and so on when dressing up.

• Arrange a 'crazy day' when all the children come to the setting dressed in 'crazy clothes' that they have chosen for themselves at home that morning (let children not able to dress-up at home choose clothes from the role-play area). Take a photo of each child and display them for everyone to see. The children can enjoy discussing what they are wearing.

Let's talk!

Ask, *What did you need help with when dressing? In what order did you put on your clothes?* For children requiring support, ask *Did you get dressed by yourself today?* For children needing challenge, ask *Can you fasten your shoes?* Note children who can select and dress themselves independently in the role-play area.

A UNIQUE CHILD

POSITIVE RELATIONSHIPS

Top tip

Include clothing from various cultures and backgrounds wherever possible. Ask parents to bring in any special clothes worn for celebrations or ceremonies to share with the group.

Differentiation

Keep clothing fastenings simple for children requiring more support and be aware of trailing ties and hems. Challenge children to sort the clothes into two laundry baskets – small and large or summer and winter clothing, for example.

Further ideas

• Give each child a copy of the activity sheet 'Washing line' (photocopy page 27 or print from the CD-ROM) and decorate the clothes with patterns.

Washing line

Decorate the clothes with a pattern – stripes, dots, flowers or zig-zags.

Tidy time

Setting up

Provide an adult-sized apron with a pocket on the front and write 'I help to tidy up' on it using a marker pen. Hang it on a hook in a prominent place where the children can reach easily into the pocket.

Getting started

- Talk to the children about how they help at home. Do they throw rubbish in the bin or tidy their toys away? Discuss why it is important to keep things tidy. Explain that you are going to show the children how to take turns to tidy up in your setting. Use the pictures provided on the activity sheet 'I help to tidy up' (photocopy page 29 or print from the CD-ROM) and ask the children to colour them in and then glue them on to cards. Place the cards in the apron pocket. Explain that this apron is called the 'magic apron' because things get tidied up when a card is removed.
- At the end of a play session choose six children and, one at a time, invite them to take a card from the 'magic apron' pocket. The children then tidy up the area shown on the card. They can choose a friend to help them if they wish. As the children are busy tidying up, encourage them to discuss the position of the items, such as *Put the book next to that one* or *Where does this piece of puzzle fit?*

Let's talk!

Ask, *What goes above the crayons? Can you sort all the bricks into this box and all the play people into that box?* For children needing support, ask *Where does this go?* With children requiring challenge, observe use of positional language when tidying up the various areas of the setting.

Top tip

Ask parents to encourage their child to help with tidying up in the home. Be sensitive to the fact that children's homes will vary in their interpretation of tidiness.

Differentiation

Pair children who need more support with a child who can help them to tidy. Challenge children by drawing around the shapes of items on shelves in the role-play area so that they can match the outlines.

Further ideas

- Sing a tidying-up song to the tune of 'Frere Jacques':

  Time to tidy up, time to tidy up
  We can help, we can help
  Put the toys away, put the toys away
  Then sit down, then sit down.

books

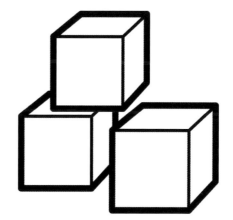

bricks

puzzles

role-play area

sand area

water area

I play with my toys

Early learning goal

Recognise and explore how sounds can be changed, sing simple songs from memory, recognise repeated sounds and sound patterns and match movements to music.

Setting up

Collect toys which make a noise, such as rattles, small musical instruments, whistles, squeaky toys, talking dolls and vehicles with sirens, and place them in a box outdoors.

Getting started

• Talk to the children about the toys they play with at home. Do they have any toys that make a noise? Can they say what they are? Look at the photo 'Playing an instrument' on the CD-ROM and talk about other instruments they enjoy playing. Gather the children in a circle and show them the collection of noisy toys and listen to the different types of sound that they make. Discuss whether the sounds are high or low, loud or soft, fast or slow. Ask the children to try and describe the noise (rattling, tinkling, ringing and so on) and compare the different sounds. Let the children enjoy playing freely with the noisy toys.

• Choose a child to sit in the centre of the circle and either blindfold them or ask them to keep their eyes tightly closed. Select another child sitting in the circle to take one of the toys and produce the sound it makes. The blindfolded child then tries to guess the toy. If they guess correctly, the child who made the sound is then blindfolded and the game continues until all the children have had a turn.

Let's talk!

Ask, *Do you have a toy at home that makes a noise? Can you make the sound of this toy with your voice?* For children requiring support, ask *How can you make a noise using this toy?* For children needing challenge, ask *Can you describe the noise of the toy you are holding?* Watch for children who can hear the difference between loud and soft sounds and high and low sounds.

Top tip

Ask parents if they could let their child bring a toy that makes a noise to share with the rest of the group. Make sure that toys are easily identified with the child's name and kept safely.

Differentiation

Use six easily identifiable noisy toys with children who need more support and provide clues if necessary. Challenge children to find spaces around the outdoor area – a blindfolded child can guess where the child is standing from the noise they make with their toy.

Further ideas

• Hide six of the noisy toys behind an upturned table or blanket and produce the sounds once. Play them again with one toy missing and ask children to identify which one it is.

I help to clean

CD-ROM resources

 What shall I clean?

Early learning goals

Listen with enjoyment, and respond to stories, songs and other music, rhymes and poems and make up their own stories, songs, rhymes and poems.

 Move with confidence, imagination and in safety.

Setting up
Collect a variety of empty cleaning containers such as spray window cleaners, furniture polish and washing-up liquid bottles (ensure they are clean and safe). Also include cleaning tools, dusters, feather dusters, sponges, cloths, dustpan and brush, small brooms and carpet sweepers.

Getting started
- Discuss with the children the various ways that their home is kept clean. Who does particular jobs in their house? Show the children the collection of cleaning items and ask them to say what is used for cleaning windows, washing dirty dishes or cleaning the carpets. Bring a vacuum cleaner to your setting and let the children take turns to help you vacuum the rug or carpet in the role-play area.
- Listen to the song 'What shall I clean?' on the CD-ROM and ask children to join in with appropriate actions as they sing along. Place the cleaning tools in the role-play area for the children to play with and suggest that they sing the rhyme as they use the tools to pretend to clean the house. See if they can use the duster to make circular motions while cleaning windows, pushing backwards and forwards when vacuuming, swinging a mop from side to side while cleaning the floor and so on.

Let's talk!
Ask, *Do you help to clean in your home? What do you do to help? Can you show me how you would polish the table?* For children requiring more support, ask *Can you show me how you clean the windows?* For children requiring challenge, ask *Can you sing the song all the way through, with all the actions?* Note individual children who respond to the song and the level of involvement they show in the activity.

Top tip
Respect those who are less confident about joining in with songs and movement. Show support and encouragement and try to make the activity fun and enjoyable by including adults who will join in enthusiastically.

Differentiation
Play alongside children who need more support, singing along with the song and suggesting movements if necessary. Ask children who require more challenge to make up their own verses to add to the song.

Further ideas
- Use child-sized brooms, rakes and dustpans and brushes to clean the outdoor area.
- Wash and clean toys indoors in the water tray and wheeled toys outdoors with a bucket and sponge.

I eat my meals

Early learning goal

 Recognise the importance of keeping healthy, and those things which contribute to this.

Setting up

Set up a large table covered with a plastic tablecloth, plastic plates and knives, wooden kebab skewers and a variety of fruit and vegetables (choose vegetables which can be eaten raw, such as cauliflower and carrots). Look at the photo 'Fruit stall' on the CD-ROM and talk about all the different types of fruit on display.

Getting started

- Home is where most of the children will have their meals. Look at the film clip of a family enjoying a mealtime on the CD-ROM. Ask children to say what they had for breakfast that morning. Who prepares most of the meals in their home? Examine your collection of fruit and vegetables with the children, observing the colour and texture, and tell the children that they are going to use them to make kebabs. Talk about how fruit and vegetables are good to eat and can help to keep us healthy.

- Discuss the importance of keeping hands and surfaces clean and the safety aspects of using knives. Then help the children to cut the fruit and vegetables into bite-sized pieces and place them on the plastic plates. Invite them to select pieces of fruit or vegetable and thread them along a skewer. Encourage them to make patterns as they do so, either by colour, size or whether they are a fruit or a vegetable.

Let's talk!

Ask, *What is your favourite fruit or vegetable? How many grapes have you put on your kebab?* With children needing support, ask *What colour are the pieces of fruit?* For children needing challenge, ask *Which are the pieces of fruit on your kebab and which are pieces of vegetable?* Look out for children who understand why eating fruit and vegetables is more healthy for them than eating chocolate or crisps.

Top tip

Find out whether any children have particular food allergies or dietary restrictions before starting this activity. Promote independence in every child in handwashing and when pushing the food on to their skewer, having set clear safety rules such as pointing the skewer away from them.

Differentiation

Cut up the food for children who require more support and help when threading pieces on the skewer. For children who require more challenge let them use knives other than plastic, under careful supervision, and develop a respect for the potential dangers involved.

Further ideas

- Take a small group of children to a local shop to buy the fruit and vegetables for this activity.

I play in my garden

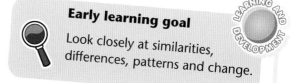

Early learning goal

Look closely at similarities, differences, patterns and change.

Setting up

Gather some bowls containing gravel, stones, compost, pieces of sponge, bark, twigs, moss, newspaper, seeds and bulbs and place them outdoors.

Getting started

- Talk to the children about the different features which might be found in a garden. These could include a wall, fence, tree, hedge, grass, pond, paving slabs, garden furniture, plant pots, gravel, soil, bushes and flowers, a shed and so on. Gather the children in the outdoor area and ask them to look carefully and identify which features they can see. Talk about seeds, flowers, trees and grass which need sunshine, water and soil to grow. Do the children think seeds will grow in anything but soil?

- Give each child a foil pie plate and suggest that they make a 'mini-garden'. Let some of the children plant seeds and bulbs in their plate using compost while others sprinkle seeds on damp sponges, newspaper and so on. They can then choose other items from the bowls and arrange them in the plate to represent rocks, trees and ornamental features. Add the seed packet to a stick and place it in the mini-garden to remind the children of what they planted.

- Place the mini-gardens together in a sunny place and make sure that the children water them regularly. Observe them every day, noting any changes which take place and invite the children to record them with a camera. Display the photos indoors in sequence. Encourage the children to click on the interactive picture 'In the garden' on the CD-ROM and watch the garden change throughout the seasons.

Top tip

Be aware that many children don't have gardens to play in but explain that flowers can be grown in all sorts of containers. Ask parents with gardens to let their child help them to look after it. Use seeds which are easy to grow.

Differentiation

Provide suggestions for children who require more support in arranging their gardens and supervise the watering activity every day. Challenge children to record their observations on paper and create a book showing the growth of their mini-garden.

Further ideas

- Grow carrot-top gardens in the foil pie plates. Cut the tops off carrots and place them in about 1cm of water.

My neighbourhood   Our street

Early learning goal

Observe, find out about and identify features in the place they live and the natural world.

Setting up
With parents' permission take small groups of children on a walk around the local neighbourhood. Discuss the importance of road safety. Let the children suggest specific landmarks to photograph along the way that can be easily recognised, such as a letterbox, zebra crossing, road signs, churches and other buildings of interest.

Getting started
- Look at the pictures taken on the walk and ask if the children can name the various buildings and features. Can they remember in which order they saw them? Spread an old white sheet on a large table or on the ground and tape it down securely. Using felt marker pens, draw a simple representation of your setting together with the local streets.
- Ask the children to paint the landmarks shown on the photos in the correct place on the map and then add houses, shops, parks and playgrounds and any other aspects of the neighbourhood. Include natural features such as hills, streams or ponds. When the map is complete, introduce small world people, wooden trees and toy cars and invite the children to play with them as they find their way along the streets. Challenge them to drive the cars along the shortest route to your setting, walk to the local park, post a letter and so on.

Let's talk!
Ask, *Where did we cross the road? Can you tell a friend how to get to the local shop?* For children needing more support, ask *How can I find our nursery?* For challenge, ask children if they can tell the difference between moveable and non-moveable landmarks. Note children who can use geographical terms such as 'street', 'house', 'church' and use these during their play.

Top tip
Include features, houses and places of religion which represent all the children in the local community. Note those children who can recognise the different cultures of the people who live in the same community.

Differentiation
Help children who need more support to place photos of buildings on their map, rather than drawing them. Challenge children to make other maps on large sheets of paper, such as a map to show the route of the Gingerbread Man.

Further ideas
- Encourage the children to click on the interactive picture 'Street scene' on the CD-ROM.
- Ask a local road safety officer to visit and provide some appropriate resources.

Tidy neighbourhood

Early learning goals

 Understand what is right, what is wrong, and why.

 Find out about their environment, and talk about those features they like and dislike.

Setting up

Listen to the song 'Put it in the bin!' on the CD-ROM and sing it with the children. Take the children, with parental permission, on a walk in the local area. Ask the children to wear plastic gloves and give each one a bag in which to collect any litter they find (under supervision). Ask the children to bring in any old cardboard boxes and tubes from home.

Getting started

- Tip the rubbish collected on to a large sheet and look at the things people have thrown away. Decide which of these items could be recycled, without touching. Discuss other things that we might throw away, such as newspapers, uneaten food, tins, bottles, food wrappers and vegetable peelings.

- Gather the boxes together and examine them with the children, discussing the size and shape. Invite them to join the boxes and tubes together using glue or tape to make sculptures such as space cities, trains, animals or monsters. Let the children paint their box sculptures and, when dry, glue on any collage materials. Thread string through the sculptures and hang them around the setting or varnish them and hang them outdoors from tree branches or fences for the children to enjoy.

Let's talk!

Ask, *Why is it wrong to throw litter on the ground?* For children who need more support, ask *What have you made with your junk boxes?*
For those who need challenge, ask *What do you think was kept in the boxes you used for your sculpture?*
Observe those children who can distinguish between different types of rubbish and can recycle correctly.

Top tip

Take plenty of adult helpers with you on your walks and take the opportunity to talk to the children about what they see. Make sure that the children know it is important not to pick up glass or sharp objects and supervise carefully at all times.

Differentiation

Provide assistance for children who need support when joining the boxes together to ensure the sculptures are sturdy. For challenge, ask children to make two or more smaller sculptures from rubbish and string them together.

Further ideas

- Provide three plastic bins labelled with the pictures and captions 'uneaten food', 'cans and bottles' and 'wrappings' for the children to sort their food into at snack and lunchtimes.
- Provide examples of rubbish which could be thrown away and ask children to decide which could be recycled, put in the compost or sent to a charity shop.

My friends

Setting up

In the outdoor play area set up an obstacle course to represent a street, with activities which require working in pairs. Include balancing obstacles, a row of tyres, a square 'chalk house' drawn on the ground, stepping stone mats, cones to walk down a 'street', something to climb over (smooth branches or poles) and a climbing frame 'house'. Look at the video 'Children at play' on the CD-ROM and talk about playing with friends and the interests they share.

Getting started

- Talk to the children about any friends they have who live near them and come to their home to play. Ask the children to take turns naming their best friend. What activities do they do together? Give each child a copy of the activity sheet 'For my friend' (photocopy page 37 or print from the CD-ROM) and ask them to draw a picture for a friend.
- Show the children the obstacles outside and explain that they must choose a friend and take turns to help each other around the course. Let them hold hands and support their friend as they walk along a balance beam, around the chalk lines of the house and negotiate the street of cones. Explain how they can support their partner as they jump from one stepping-stone to another or climb over the hurdles or climbing frame. Invite the children to take turns to wear a blindfold and lead each other safely around the obstacles, giving instructions to guide them.

Let's talk!

Ask, *How did you help your friend to jump along the stepping stones?* For children who require more support, ask *Did your friend help you to walk along the balance beam?* For children who need challenge, ask *Can you close your eyes and let your friend guide you through the cones?*

Top tip

Try to ensure that the children develop care and trust in their partner and understand that their partner should have the same trust in them. Support and reassure less confident children, with an adult to act as their partner if necessary.

Differentiation

Invite children who need more support to use a mobility aid to play 'follow my leader' with their friend, helping each other as they move around the chalk house or along ropes on the ground. Children who require challenge can create their own pathways, considering the space required for themselves and a partner.

Further ideas

- Use mats, hoops and tyres to make a trail and ask the children to work their way along without touching the ground with the help of their friend.

For my friend

To my friend ...

I like my friend
And when we play
I try to be kind
In every way

From your friend ...

Going to school

CD-ROM resources

I went to school one morning

Going to school game

Early learning goal

Talk about, recognise and recreate simple patterns.

Setting up

Set up the outdoor area with large and small wooden and plastic building bricks, light planks, poles (bamboo or garden sticks), skipping ropes and washing lines. Create a representation of a school out of a large cardboard box, climbing frame covered with blankets or large building blocks.

Getting started

- Talk to the children about how they travel to the setting, whether they walk, travel by car, taxi or bus or ride in a pushchair. Listen to the song 'I went to school one morning' on the CD-ROM and then sing along. Look at large-scale maps of the local area (such as those provided by a local tourist information office) and look for well-known features.
- Gather the children together outdoors and explain that you are going to make routes to the school using the equipment provided. Encourage the children to work together while making the roads. They can make them straight and winding, turning around corners, zig-zagging or up and down inclines as long as they all finish at the model of the setting. Invite the children to hop, skip, run or jump along the paths as they sing the song 'I went to school one morning'.
- Introduce large dolls and soft toys for the children to walk along the paths while playing outdoors. See if the children can tell stories about their journey, suggesting things that their doll might see on the way to school.

Let's talk!

Ask, *What did you use to make your path? How did you move along the path?* For children requiring more support, ask *Can you show me the way you travelled?* Ask children requiring challenge if they can explain the directions a doll should take to travel to school. Listen to those children who use language such as *curved*, *straight*, *corner* or *turn left at the zebra crossing* during their play.

Top tip

Give children sufficient time to explore the outdoor environment and make patterns while creating their roads and paths. Encourage them to use problem-solving skills when encountering any natural obstacles in their way.

Differentiation

Let children who need more support work alongside an older, more able child or adult to help them move the equipment as necessary. Children who need more challenge can add features such as a river and bridge, T-junction or a tunnel (using a play tunnel or blanket draped over a table) to their route.

Further ideas

- Play the 'Going to school' game (photocopy page 39 or print from the CD-ROM).

Going to school game

A game for two children. Use counters and a dice.

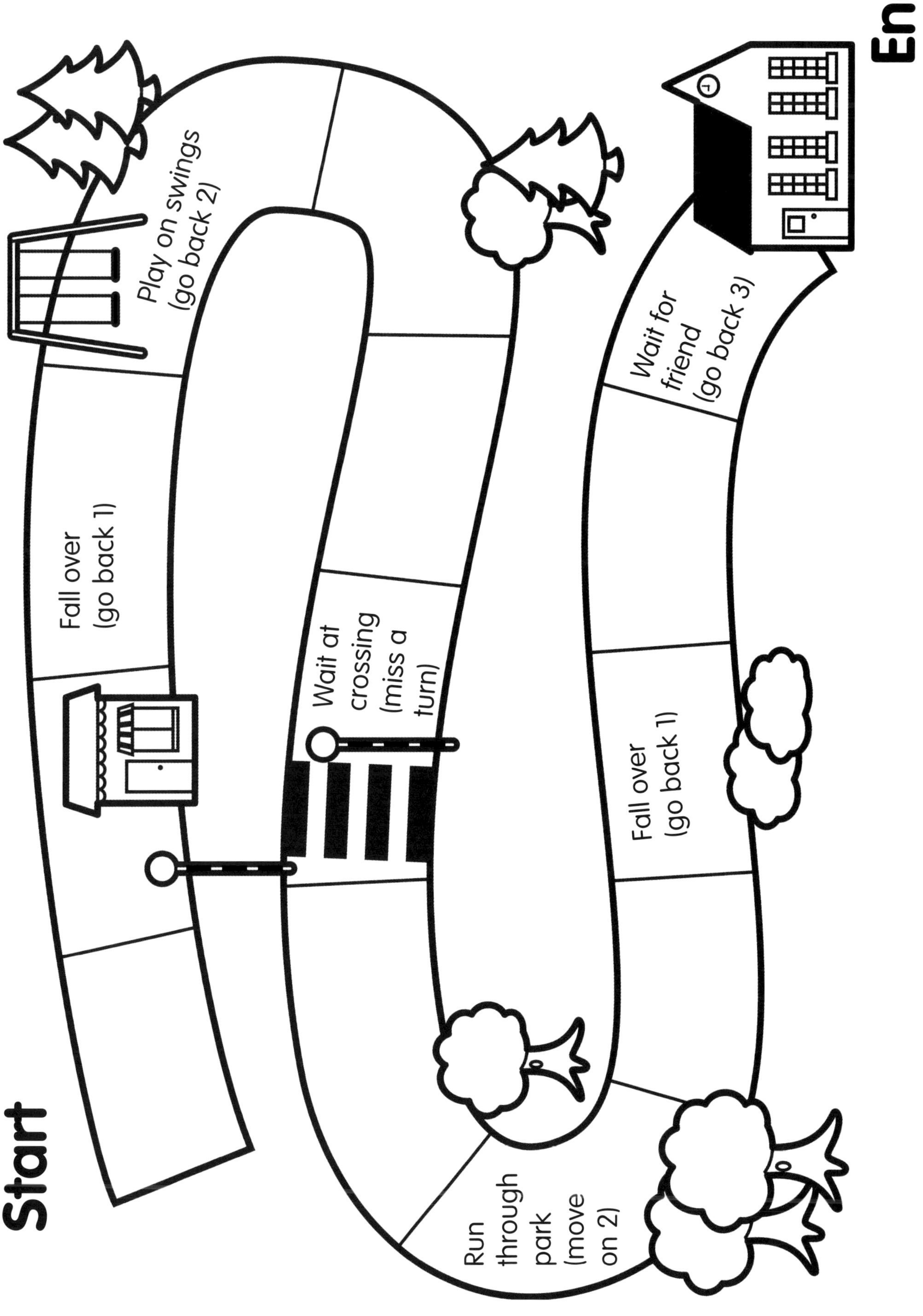

Start

End

Play on swings (go back 2)

Fall over (go back 1)

Wait at crossing (miss a turn)

Wait for friend (go back 3)

Fall over (go back 1)

Run through park (move on 2)

People around us

Early learning goals

Sustain attentive listening, responding to what they have heard with relevant comments, questions or actions.

Use their imagination in art and design, music, dance, imaginative and role-play and stories.

Setting up

Collect together two or three objects (real or toy versions) which represent the jobs done by various people who live in the area (stethoscope, bandages, fluorescent jacket and cap, police officer's helmet, hard hat and so on). Keep them all together in a play sack. Look at the photo 'Police officer' on the CD-ROM and talk about what he is wearing and what he might be doing.

Getting started

- Focus the children's attention on those people in their community who they might meet. These could include the local doctor or nurse, crossing warden, police officer, builder, market trader, librarian and postman. Discuss the type of job they do and how they help us. Arrange a 'people around us' week and invite a different community helper to visit the group each day. Ask the children to sit and listen carefully as they talk about their job. Encourage them to ask questions about what they have heard and then thank their visitor for coming to talk to them. Take a photo of each visitor and make these into a book entitled 'People around us' for the children to enjoy in the story corner.
- Point out those tools in the play sack that the nurse might use and let the children play with them in the role-play area. At the end of the week look at all the equipment collected, identifying who might use a particular item and encourage children to re-enact the different jobs during their play.

Let's talk!

Ask, *What did the librarian talk about when she came for a visit?* For children requiring more support, ask *How did the road safety officer tell you to cross the road safely?* For children requiring challenge, ask when they might need a fire officer. Note which children use the book to recall the people who visited and the jobs they do.

Top tip

Children may have different experiences when coming into contact with adults in various positions in the local community. Encourage them to share their experiences, on a one-to-one basis if necessary.

Differentiation

Encourage children who need more support to sit attentively in small groups and listen quietly to their visitor. Suggest questions that they could ask. For challenge, ask children to write a short thank you note to their visitors.

Further ideas

- Set up the role-play area to represent a dentist or doctor's surgery, library or post office.

Traffic on our street

Early learning goals

Respond in a variety of ways to what they see, hear, smell, touch and feel.

Setting up

Look at the photo 'A busy street' on the CD-ROM and talk about the different kinds of traffic. Read books and poems with the children about different types of transport. Take the children, with parental permission, on short walks to watch the traffic near your setting and identify the vehicles which drive past. Emphasise the road safety aspect.

Getting started

- Talk about the different types of vehicles the children might see on the roads around their home. Ask them to collect an assortment of old small world wheeled vehicles which represent those they saw while 'traffic watching' and place them in a tray near a table prepared for painting. Place a thin layer of different paint colours (three or four) in trays on the table and show the group how to dip the wheels of a toy vehicle carefully in the paint and then roll it around their sheet of paper. They can then 'drive' another vehicle dipped in a different coloured paint around the paper.
- Encourage the children to make interesting shapes and patterns, criss-crossing the wheel-marks over each other. Draw attention to the size of the tyres and the tracks they make. When the paintings are dry, let the children drive the vehicles around the roads that they have made, perhaps with accompanying *brum-brum* noises that they heard while looking at the traffic on the street. Display the pictures for them to compare the colours and patterns.

Let's talk!

Ask, *Can you remember how many wheels you saw on the motorbike? Which vehicle has the biggest wheels? What do you think made those tracks?* For children requiring more support, ask *Can you follow the red wheel-marks around your painting?* For children needing more challenge, ask *How can you tell which tracks are made by bigger vehicles?* Find out which children use the experience of watching traffic when using vehicles in the painting activity.

Top tip

Show an interest in every child's response to the traffic they see and appreciate all the creations made by them as a result. Listen to their individual experiences of travel in various road vehicles.

Differentiation

Show children who require more support how to cover the wheels using a paint-soaked sponge to obtain the best tracks. For children who require challenge, try out different types of paint by adding glue or sawdust. Does runny or thick paint make the best tracks?

Further ideas

- Make puddles of water in the outdoor area and ride wheeled toys through to create tyre tracks.

Where do I live? Castles in the air

CD-ROM resources

Jack and the giant

Jack and the giant's clothes

Early learning goals

Use their imagination in art and design, music, dance, imaginative and role-play and stories.

Use language such as 'circle' or 'bigger' to describe the shape and size of solids and flat shapes.

Setting up

Listen to the story 'Jack and the giant' on the CD-ROM. Collect a variety of clothes in two sizes, one size as large as you can find and another child-sized.

Getting started

- Talk to the children about the story of Jack and the giant. Discuss the size of the giant and what sort of clothes he might wear. Where could he buy giant-sized clothes? Gather the children together and look at the clothes you have collected. Have fun trying them on and deciding which would fit the giant and which would fit Jack. Use language such as *too big, too small, just the right size* and so on as the children compare the sizes of the clothes.
- Place the clothes in the role-play area and invite the children to use them in their play as they take on the roles of Jack or the giant. Add large and small bowls, spoons and chairs and let the children decide who would use each one. Create props such as the five apple seeds and the bag of gold to help the children re-enact the story of Jack and the giant during their play.

Let's talk!

Ask, *Can you show me the clothes you think the giant would wear? Do you think this would fit you or the giant?* For children who need more support, ask *Can you pick up a giant-sized pair of shoes?* For children who require challenge, ask *Can you sort the clothes into large and small sizes?* Note those children who use narrative from the story in their play.

Top tip

Respect those children who are less confident by playing alongside them, introducing storylines and the *Fee, fi, fo, fum* narrative as necessary and using appropriate language.

Differentiation

Help children who need more support to dress up in the clothes and ensure that there is a clear difference in the sizes. Provide duvets, blankets and pillows in large and small sizes for children who require challenge to make large and small beds in the role-play area suitable for Jack and the giant to sleep in.

Further ideas

- Move like Jack and the giant to suitable music, with large, giant strides and small running steps.
- Give each child a copy of the activity sheet 'Jack and the giant's clothes' (photocopiable page 43 or print from the CD-ROM).

Jack and the giant's clothes

Draw lines to match the clothes with the owner.

I live in the sea

CD-ROM resources

I am swimming

Under the sea

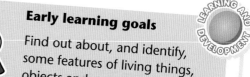
Early learning goals

Find out about, and identify, some features of living things, objects and events they observe.

Count reliably up to ten everyday objects.

Setting up
Set up the water tray outdoors, add blue food colouring to represent the sea and place seashells and small rocks in the bottom. Collect several different kinds of plastic fish, sharks, and so on in various colours and sizes. Share books and pictures of creatures that live in the sea.

Getting started
- Talk to the children about the various creatures that live under the sea. Show the children a small, whole fish from a fishmongers and look at the eyes, mouth, gills, fins and tail. Draw the children's attention to the scales that cover the fish and let them experience what they feel like with their fingers. *What does the fish smell like?* Place the fish on a pair of scales and find out how heavy it is. Be sure that everyone washes their hands afterwards and talk about hygiene issues.
- Place the plastic fish in the water tray and let the children wear sunglasses and beach hats as they try to catch them using children's fishing nets. Encourage the group to count how many fish they have caught and discuss the size and colours.
- Listen to the rhyme 'I am swimming' on the CD-ROM and encourage the children to move around outdoors as suggested by the names of the different sea creatures.

Let's talk!
Ask, *What does the real fish feel like? Can you show me the biggest fish you have caught?* For children who need more support, ask *What colour is that fish you have caught?* For children who require challenge, ask *What do you think lived in this shell? What do fish use to breathe with under the water?* Note which children are curious and show an interest in finding out more about fish. Do they ask questions and talk about what they have discovered?

Top tip
Include parents or staff who have any particular knowledge of fish (a fisherman or owner of a tropical fish tank, for example) in this activity.

Differentiation
Provide suggestions for octopus, shark or turtle movements when listening to the 'I am swimming' rhyme for children who need more support. For children who need challenge, set a timer and let two children see who can catch the most fish within a certain period.

Further ideas
- Encourage the children to click on the interactive picture 'Under the sea' on the CD-ROM and match the pairs of fish.

Cave homes

CD-ROM resources

Brown bear and cubs

Early learning goals

Move with control and coordination.

Listen with enjoyment, and respond to stories, songs and other music, rhymes and poems and make up their own stories, songs, rhymes and poems.

Setting up

Share some books and poems about bears with the children. Set up the sand tray outdoors with a good thickness of damp sand and a selection of plastic spiders, bears, dragons and small world people.

Getting started

- Read *We're Going on a Bear Hunt* by Michael Rosen (Walker Books). Discuss what the children found in the cave at the end of their walk. Explain to the children that bears often sleep through the winter in a cave and emerge in the spring. Look at the photo 'Brown bear and cubs' on the CD-ROM and talk about what bears look like. Explain that people very long ago made their homes in caves. Talk about other creatures that might live in a cave: spiders, dragons and so on.
- Ask the children if they can make caves in the sand. Suggest that they use their hands rather than a spade so that their cave will not collapse. Let the children play with the small world people and animals and see if they can place them carefully in their caves. Say the following finger rhyme with the children:

> *Here is a cave* (bend fingers over on one hand)
> *What is inside?*
> *I think it's a bear* (put thumb inside fingers)
> *And he's trying to hide!* (cover 'bear' with fingers)
> *He sleeps through the winter*
> *While snow is about* (lay other hand flat over cave)
> *But watch out, it's spring*
> *And the bear's coming out!* (pop out thumb)

Let's talk!

Ask, *Can you tell me how you made your cave?* For children who require support, ask *Can you hide that spider in your cave?* For children who require challenge, ask *Can you build a cave big enough for six bears to sleep in?* Notice those children who can manipulate the sand and use vocabulary for the processes.

Top tip

Encourage all the children to devise their own way of building sand caves, whatever their ability, and praise all efforts. Ensure that everyone has the opportunity to express their imagination.

Differentiation

Show children who need support how to bank the sand into a corner of the sand tray and pat it down firmly so that it is easier to dig out a cave. Ask children who require challenge if they can make caves in the sand which interlink through tunnels.

Further ideas

- Provide teddy bears and dolls in the role-play area and make caves using blankets to re-enact stories and songs.

Homes in cold places

Setting up

Set up the water tray outdoors with plastic trays, a supply of ice cubes and plastic small world people.

Getting started

- Talk to the group about homes around the world. Draw the children's attention to homes in hot countries that have very thick walls or need air-conditioning to keep cool, tall skyscrapers or houses on stilts over water. What might it be like to live in a very cold country? Watch the film clip of husky dogs on the CD-ROM. Talk about the snow and why constant ice and snow on the road mean people sometimes use sleighs (like Santa). Explain that in some very cold countries homes are made of snow and called igloos. They keep people warm in freezing areas like the Arctic. Find some examples in books to share with the group.

- Explain to the children that they can make ice houses using ice cubes. Place lots of ice cubes on the trays. If you put different food colouring in the water before you freeze the cubes the children can have a colourful house. Let the children play with the ice cubes, building an igloo that gets smaller towards the top with an opening around the base. If they sprinkle the cubes with a little salt it will help them to stick together. When they have finished playing with the ice cubes invite the children to tip them into the water tray and watch them melt.

Let's talk!

Ask, *Would you like to live in a cold country? What would you wear if you lived in an ice house?* For children requiring more support, ask *What do the ice cubes feel like?* For children requiring challenge, ask *What happens when the ice cubes melt?* Note those children who can use language such as *freezing*, *melt*, *icy*, *slippery* or *smooth* when describing their experience.

Top tip

Use care with ice cubes straight from the freezer. The children can wear gloves or use small pairs of tongs. Encourage those with knowledge of homes in different parts of the world to share their experiences with the rest of the group.

Differentiation

For children requiring more support let them build simple square houses with the ice cubes, placing them carefully one on top of the other. For children who require challenge make larger ice blocks by freezing water in yogurt pots for them to build houses with.

Further ideas

- Make larger ice blocks by freezing water in ice cream or margarine containers and make ice houses outdoors.

I live in a shoe

Early learning goal

Count reliably up to ten everyday objects.

Setting up

Make a selection of different types of shoes (include adult and child-sized shoes, sports shoes, boots, wellingtons, slippers and so on). Draw a very large shoe on paper with a door and lots of windows. Cut around three sides of the door and windows then fold them back to open and close. Glue small envelopes behind the windows to create pockets which could hold pieces of card. Display the shoe on the wall at child height.

Getting started

- Discuss the shoe collection with the children. Talk about the different types of fastenings, colours and times when we need to wear a particular type of shoe. Familiarise the children with the rhyme 'There was an old woman who lived in a shoe' and ask them what sort of shoe they would choose to live in. Listen to the 'Big shoe song' on the CD-ROM and sing along.

- Ask the group to draw lots of small images of children on pieces of card and colour them in. Cut out the figures and invite the children to use them when playing with the shoe house you made earlier. Ask the children to place the figures in the windows (the envelopes attached behind the window openings will provide a pocket for them to sit in) and encourage them to count and use number names as they do so. See if the children can say the rhyme 'There was an old woman' as they play with the shoe.

Let's talk!

Ask, *How many children are you going to put behind this window?* For children requiring support, ask *Where are you going to put that figure? How many are behind the window now?* For children needing challenge, ask *How many children has the old woman got living in her shoe altogether?* Note those children who are willing to attempt counting and use number names while playing with the shoe. Do they count and compare numbers?

Top tip

Participate in play to encourage the use of number language and counting with the children. Support those children who use a language other than English in their understanding of counting.

Differentiation

Cut out the figures for children requiring more support and limit the number to no more than 10, depending upon counting ability. Let children requiring challenge play with figures of up to 20 or more and begin to 'take away' figures from groups and find out how many are left.

Further ideas

- Let the children find out how many small world figures will fit into a variety of shoes such as a man's shoe, a wellington boot or child's shoe.

Gingerbread house

CD-ROM resources

Gingerbread house

Early learning goals

Work as part of a group or class, taking turns and sharing fairly, understanding that there needs to be agreed values and codes of behaviour for groups of people, including adults and children, to work together harmoniously.

Use language such as 'circle' or 'bigger' to describe the shape and size of solids and flat shapes.

Setting up

Set up a food preparation area with simple food which can be used to create edible houses: crackers, cheese slices (whole and halved into triangles), slices of bread, gingerbread biscuits, pretzels, slices of cucumber (round and cut into squares), apple shapes, carrot sticks, grapes. Place the ingredients on paper plates. Discuss any children who may have allergies or dietary restrictions with parents before this activity.

Getting started

- Read the traditional story of 'Hansel and Gretel' and discuss how the witch's house was made of food that is nice to eat. Look at the photo 'Gingerbread house' on the CD-ROM and talk about what it might be made of. Explain to the children that they are going to make a house to eat. Remind them about washing hands before they start.
- Invite the children, one at a time, to take a paper plate and select food with which to arrange a house on their plate. They may, for example, choose to use a square cracker as the house, or a large cheese slice cut in half as the roof and a rectangular piece of apple to represent the door. Encourage them to make their own choices. Involve the children in agreeing behaviour such as taking turns when selecting their food; only taking the pieces they require thus leaving food for others to share and not to touch food other than the items they choose. Suggest that they could share their ideas for making houses with the rest of the group.

Let's talk!

Ask, *Whose turn is it now to make a house snack?* For children needing support, ask *Can you tell your friend what food you have chosen to make your house?* For children requiring challenge, ask *What can you use for a chimney if the last pretzel has gone?* Observe those children who can demonstrate flexibility and understand the concept of turn-taking.

Top tip

Use food which reflects a variety of ethnic backgrounds and cultures familiar to the children.

Differentiation

Encourage children needing support to wait their turn and to ask for help. Children requiring challenge can take photos of the snacktime houses they create.

Further ideas

- Make a ladybird to eat by setting red jelly in an oval mould. After turning it out, decorate with chocolate buttons for spots.